Taking Down the Angel

BOOKS BY JEFF FRIEDMAN

The Record-Breaking Heat Wave
Scattering the Ashes
Taking Down the Angel

Taking Down the Angel

Poems by Jeff Friedman

Carnegie Mellon University Press
Pittsburgh 2003

ACKNOWLEDGMENTS

My thanks to the editors of the following publications in which these poems
first appeared:

The 2River View: "The Squatters" and "Rain"

The Alembic: "My Father out of the Wind," "Bowling Instruction," and
    "Manifest Destiny"

Boulevard: "The Field Behind the Old NuWay Cleaners"

Crab Orchard Review: "In the Kingdom of My Palm"

Columbia: A Journal of Literature and Art: "Orpheus in Williamsburg"

Descant: "Recital" and "The Bitterness of the Prophet"

5 AM: "1965, Dusk"

Graham House Review: "Jacob"

Granite Review: "Burial at the River"

The Heartlands Today: "Working the Loading Dock at Famous-Barr" and
    "On the Riverfront"

Kerem: "King David"

Manoa: "Two Salesmen"

Midstream: "Joseph"

Mystic River Review: "Walking"

Natural Bridge: "Burp Water" and "Finding the Action"

New Millennium Writings: "Conversation"

New Virginia Review: "Poem for Larry Levis"

Pleiades: "Mr. Clark's Last Class"

Press: "Heat Wave," "Miss Strong and I," "Stardust, 1967," "Marvin Miller Gets
    His Shirts," and "Learning to Sell Fuller Brush"

River Styx: "First Job"

The Rocky Mountain Review: "Learning to Box"

Virtual Word: "Vigil"

The Worcester Review: "On the Banks of the Mascoma"

"Finding the Action" was awarded the 1998 Milton Dorfman Poetry Prize.
"Jacob" was selected for *The Best of the Graham House Review*.

I wish to thank *Poetry Magazine. com*, *PoetryTonight.com* and *Valparaiso Poetry Review* for
reprinting a number of my poems. I wish also to thank the Yaddo Corporation and the
Vermont Studio Center for their generous support. My special thanks to William
Doreski, Jack Driscoll, Donald Finkel, Ken Smith, Marcia Southwick, Ellen Geist,
Charna Meyers, Sharon Dolin, Chard de Niord, Howard Schwartz and Colleen Randall
for their support and encouragement and for their help with this collection of poems.

The publication of this book is supported by a grant from the
Pennsylvania Council on the Arts.

Book design: Cassandra Knight

Library of Congress Control Number 2002101668

ISBN 0-88748-400-X

ISBN 0-88748-384-4 Pbk.

10 9 8 7 6 5 4 3 2

CONTENTS

ONE

TWO

THREE

FOR MY MOTHER

ONE

MY FATHER OUT OF THE WIND

My father comes to me as a little
bit of dust swirling in the wind.
He no longer slumps when he walks
or scrapes his heels on the pavement
as he lugs his two beaten canvas grips.
He is no longer anxious
and tired, stretching his hairy arms toward
the ceiling and crumpling into a
loud slumber in his chair. He has
survived yet another Egypt
and a thousand Pharoahs. He comes
to me as a little bit of dust
that flares in the wind like a swarm of locusts.
I see his bearded face, born in the
time of Isaac, streaked with tears.
He has survived the gnashing of teeth,
the punishing blows, the hammering hoofs
that pound the desert floor,
the violent diasporas. I hear him
rising with the ferocity of a hyena,
a gleam of light in its yellow eyes
as it crunches the neck bones of its prey.
He swirls in the air above the yellow
wildflowers in the shadow of the mountain—
a little bit of dust, some words
to the wise, an exhortation
to the wicked, a new covenant,
and his legend grows mighty on the tongues of strangers.

TWO SALESMEN
(Sunday Night, Fall 1961)

"Work hard," my uncle Harold says
"and you'll get somewhere, boy"
and my father nods his head
of black curly hair.
With drinks cradled in their hands
they sit side by side
on two throne-shaped swivel
chairs, staring at the small black
screen set in the tan console,
carved wood doors
pinned back against blond wood.

Harold sips the scotch
slowly, but my father drinks it down
then rattles the ice in his glass.
I sit on the carpet in front of them
playing solitaire Vegas-style
while they repeat the same stories,
how Galvani made a fortune
in Houston, how Klein's went
under because of bad management,
how Challoff declared bankruptcy
but not before he put away
"a pretty penny" for himself.

"I lost a 25,000-piece order,"
my father says, "because Henry
couldn't ship it on time."
"That's crazy." Harold's clipped
thick mustache tickles his
long hawkish nose
whenever he smiles or laughs.
He can make a quarter disappear
from his hands and pull it out
from behind my ear. He can shuffle
a deck in one hand
and turn over an ace of spades
anytime he wants to. I tell him
I've gone out twice in a row.
"Amazing," he says,
but my father looks down at me
with his sad tired eyes.
"Quit cheating—play it right."

Outside the wind tears at the trees
and fading red and gold,
the leaves tumble in a shower of leaves
and one more fall passes.
The wasps curl in their white
paper house shaped
like a large beautiful shell.

And the cedar bushes bunch
together like broccoli. In fall
my father died in a car accident
practically penniless
and my uncle went to sleep
forever in a hotel room
hundreds of miles from home,
staring at a picture of the sea
and three white gulls frozen on the shore.

"Work hard," Harold says
and my father nods his assent
cracking the ice between his teeth
while I cheat at solitaire
pulling a card from the bottom
of the deck when I need it
to keep my run going.
The swivel chairs squeak
and groan as my father and uncle
lean together and whisper
their plans to make it big.
Then they toast each other and touch
the empty glasses to their lips.

LEARNING TO BOX

"Always lead with your left—
never leave your chin out."
He closes my right hand
into a fist and cups it with his left

like paper wrapping rock
in Rock, Paper, Scissors.
Then he yanks it up to guard my chin.
My father has a square chin,

which is good for a man. Mine is
round. His black curly
hair tightens on his forehead.
My sandy brown hair falls

in loose strands that tickle
the skin above my eyebrows.
"Do you understand?" I nod.
While the Friday Night Fight breaks

between rounds, the Gillette jingle
plays on the tv, in the living room—
"Look sharp . . . and feel sharp . . . and be sharp—"
and a bright light drops over us,

like the light in a boxing ring, where we
stand in my room between bed and desk.
"Let me see what you know."
I get into position, crouching,

my shoulders lifted almost to my ears,
looking over my knuckles at the hump
in his white t-shirt where
his belly pushes out.

"If some guy throws a punch here,"
he says and presses his fist
against my right cheek bone,
"step inside if you can

and let him have it with your right."
He recoils his fist and drives it
toward me, turning it at the last
second near the tip of my nose,

his knuckles swollen into a knot.
I watch it as though staring through a window
at some belligerent bird
ripping a worm from the bark

trails in the trunk of a maple.
"Punch him like you mean it
and no one will ever bother you
again. . . . Do you understand?"

I nod again. Now the bell for the
10th round dings and as he turns
away, the quarters ching
in his deep loose pockets.

HEAT WAVE

My father arrives here
like a sudden wind
knocking down the leaves
of the sycamores.
He arrives on a hot
muggy night
when the dark clouds bulk
over the shingled roofs
and the rain refuses
to fall. The screen door
slams shut.
His suitcases bump
the walls and the chandelier
creaks on its chain over
the shiny formica table top.
When he enters my room
he carries the smell
of tar, asphalt,
twenty-one days
on the road, Peoria,
Decature, Dayton,
the smell of disappointment—
Lavoris on his breath,
English Leather
slapped on his cheeks,
grips in his hands.
It is the summer when
his luck turns bad,
when his sales fall
and never rise again,

when his rich friends,
who started with him in business
twenty years before,
no longer return
his calls. Under
the sheets I pretend
to be asleep though
I feel his eyes staring.
It is the summer of no
extra money to spend,
no raise in allowance,
the fan on the fritz.
All night I hear him
rise from his bed
and walk through the apartment
looking for a room
where he can rest.

RAIN

When it rains, the river plunges
over rocks and the rocks
ring like bells. Prayers
swirl in the slick street.
The sheets clipped to clotheslines
unfurl, their white targets
growing gray. The roof drips
into a crater of mud.

Mrs. Tarlick comes back to her spotless kitchen
to leaf through a *Life Magazine*
and worry over a pot of cabbage soup.
In his bear-spotted pajamas,
Al Miltie walks outside again
and pulls a glass tube from the ground
and records the moisture levels
in his hardbound blue notebook.

As my mother steps from a shiny
red and white taxicab
in her stiletto heels,
I press my nose against the window,
leave breathprints on glass,
and a black umbrella opens its ragged
wings in a bright yellow tub.

MISS STRONG AND I

When Miss Strong caught me
during our forty-five minute naptime
reading a Superboy comic
she took it from me and tore
it apart without hesitation
the way a tall skinny man
I had seen on Ed Sullivan
ripped in half a Southern Bell
White pages with his hands
and then held out both halves to the audience.

My classmates raised their heads
and looked at me with pity or contempt
except Steve Brown who had turned
his left eyelid inside out
exposing the pink insides of his eye.
Miss Strong grabbed my arm
and pulled me to the front of the class
where I was expected to stand
for the next twenty minutes
and recite the names of the first
ten presidents and tell the story
of George Washington.
Instead I predicted the spring rain

would come and wash the windows
clean (except for our thumb and noseprints)
and drench the wildflowers
and that it would splash against
the tarred blacktop until it shone
like glass. And I predicted that Miss Strong's
class would one day get better
because it couldn't get any worse.
That's enough she said and rose
again to her full height on black pumps,
her cheeks brushed with rouge
and her lips a bright red, almost
the color of her crimson blazer.

But I hadn't finished yet.
I said that in ninety days
it would be summer and we would get
out of there for good, and then I
predicted no one in his right
mind would ever marry her.
While the sun slanted through the windows
and the lights flickered
and the radiators gurgled and spit
I smelled her warm breath
and the thick scent of her perfume.

As she gripped my forearm
I predicted that she would break
all her fingernails if she didn't
stop digging them into my skin
and before too long I heard them snap
and laughed out loud until I could see
a tear squeeze from the corner
of her eye, shining as it ran down
the rutted trail of her cheek
and then I started to cry.

BOMB POPS

When I arrived
in Wentzville, the sun
beat down
hard on the tarry streets
and the dust rose
and the air broke
into shimmery waves.

Kids leaped
from the high curbs
and surrounded my truck.
I took their money
and handed them
their bomb pops
and watched them
rip off the wrappers
and toss them into the street
where they stuck in the tar.

Within moments
their faces were stained
with raspberry or chocolate
from the hard nutty
chocolate shells that covered
the malted ice cream.

On a good day
I made nearly
twenty bucks—
half of what a driver
in the city made—
riding the throne
of my truck ten
hours a day
and dreaming my future
in richer territories.

Wherever I rang my bell
they appeared
out of nowhere
with smiles on their faces
and fists squeezing
quarters, dimes, nickels, pennies.
As dragonflies arced

into the spreading leaves,
and the blue butterflies
clustered on the small
plots of lawn
disappeared into the shimmery
waves of air,
I offered my cupped
hands, waiting
to receive my reward.

LEARNING TO SELL FULLER BRUSH
(For Fred Peil)

On the porches I stood behind Ed Spoerl
and memorized his sales pitch
as I studied how he opened the screen doors
(which for him were always unlocked)
and handed each young housewife
a free basting brush.
In the bushes the locusts hummed
louder and crickets chirped
their approval. Then Ed pulled out
the monthly special,

Dust, Clean and Wax,
and sprayed it everywhere
and brought every surface
in the house to a high polish,
a hard shine in which
I could see my face clearly—
wide and crooked. Before too long,
his case was opened,
the goods spread out on a table—
the sale completed.

On my own I never got my foot
in the door. I couldn't wait
to call it quits for the day
and go to Glasers,
where girls my own age
sat at the counters
swivelling their stools
as they sipped cherry cokes
or dipped long spoons
into hot fudge sundaes.

The sun beat down hard
on my face and chest.
I mimicked Ed's sales pitch,
phrases breaking down in air to
small chunks of sound
like grains of pollen catching
the wings of birds who flew
out of there, but behind the screens
the women smiled at me
and said, "Not today."

"Then when?" I wanted to ask,
but turned away
with my Fuller Brush case
and kept ringing bells.
The one-story houses hunched
beneath the sycamores like angry frogs
ready to spring from their crouch.
The locusts clacked in the bushes.
"Not today." The street turned
tarry and stuck to my shoes.

STARDUST, 1967

Only 16 Dale Abrams and I
sat at a front table
and hit our red wood knockers
on the tabletop like the other men
and shouted for Evelyn West.

Accompanied by a long drum
roll, she strutted out
on stage in a costume of white feathers,
her 40,000 dollar treasure chest
—once insured by Lloyds of London—
only partially visible.
As she moved through a ponderous dance
she shed her feathers one by one
and tantalized and teased
and traded quips with the audience
and shot us a big smile
and called us "young peckers."

Everytime she dipped, Dale
rose to pluck a feather,
his bushy brows knit into one
long dark strip, but fell
back into his seat empty handed.
We heard the raspy voices
behind us, the chairs shifting
and scooting and the table legs groaning.
I stepped up to take a souvenir,
but she caught my hand with her sweaty palm
and shook her head and wiggled
her body and said, "Don't be naughty."

Then she bent over to show her dimples
and pointed at a large crease
on each cheek and some guy at the bar belted out,
"Hell, that's buckshot."
We chugged our rum and cokes
and watched her peel off every
last feather. For a moment,
she stood utterly naked and still.
Her face, jewelled with sweat
on forehead and chin, held
a sweetness, a glimmer of the beauty
that made her a local legend,
but the aging body sagged
and drooped, bruises spread
over her arms, chest and thighs.

The drum roll grew soft
and at last broke off. With only
one more show before closing
Evelyn West went on shaking
and jiggling her flabby breasts,
her face a wide, broad
map of boredom and worry.

We choked up with laughter
but finally turned away
and walked out into the flashing neon
of the old Grand Avenue—ashamed
as if we had just peeked through
the peephole of the bathroom door
and watched our mothers
slip off bra and panties
and display their tired, veined bodies
to the sad eyes of the mirror
and then step slowly, carefully
into the shiny white tub.

THE FIELD BEHIND THE OLD NUWAY CLEANERS

Behind the old NuWay Cleaners
where the alley turned into
blades of weeds, broken
bottles and punctured tires

laced into a mound,
a clumsy cairn,
where you could park
under the pines and cedars

and not be seen from the road
or the windows of houses on the slope,
we lay together in the back
seat of a blue Mustang. There

no train broke the silence of rusted
rails, and the smell of wild onion
and mint drifted through our windows
until our skins prickled.

In the dark blue jar
between earth and sky
the ghosts of old lovers
flared like fireflies.

The hot, muggy air
pressed its palms
against our faces while
the crickets scraping their legs

spoke dark fires
and the 7-year locusts
flung themselves into
a frenzy of sex

in mid-air, letting
their fertilized eggs
shower over the earth.
The sweet city of your hair

tumbled into darkness,
but your eyes held me
a moment longer
then let go and looked

beyond us to the small
space of sky
where desire swirled up
in a blaze of white

and vanished,
your breath a handful
of stars opening
in blue water.

BURIAL AT THE RIVER

I plant my father, a white gravel,
in water. Nothing grows, but his will
to go on selling women's wear to strangers.
Old clothes wash up, a polyester blouse,
a pair of khaki slacks, a dress
made of rayon. Catfish skim
his remains from the bottom land. In the greenish
waters pioneers fill their bellies
with German sausages and watch
fireworks flare against the sky.
The misshapen coins I toss into the river,
wrought beneath the wheels of trains,
crack rocks. I find traces of my father
in the crevices of the wharf and dig them out
with a stick. His voice jackhammers
the Eads Bridge. When smokestacks puff out,
the toy factory on the hill fails again—
the smell of glue sticking in the wind.
The river becomes a small room. On the wharf
an old woman lops off fish heads
and prepares a stew in her iron kettle.
The lightkeeper ignites a flame
in the blue globes strung
from post to post. My father's fleshy
face blinks away pain.
He unfolds the damp dollar bills
crumpled in his pocket and lays them
on the radiator one by one.

TWO

ESAU

Like my brother
I waited to skim
the fat from our father's
flock, but the sheep
lay down at our feet
and the the tiger roared
for salt.

Too late for profits, I thought
and what I got—
dirt, straw, twigs,
feathers, the husks
of shelters scattered
over the craggy terrain—
no one wanted.

Who taught the coyote
to cheat? Who taught the angels
to pray for us
with their tiresome voices?
Blue moths clung
to their heads like wrinkled leaves.

He stayed close
to home, watched over
the provisions while I
ran with beasts,
peach fuzz on the tips
of my ears, a reddish
curly beard, black fibrous
strands on my back
and fine silky chest
hair women loved
to let their fingers
slide through.

When everything turned
dark, I followed
the light of my shoes
to the table, where my birthright
waited, steaming,
shiny, swirled
my fingers through the spicy
thick stew
and cleaned my bowl.

FIRST JOB

"I'm breaking in the new boy,"
he told the cutters who came
back to the dock in their blue
aprons with requests for cloth
on small slips of paper.

Prophet of the loading dock
Jerry Gantz pointed to the alley
and predicted three trucks
would arrive by noon
and that look came over his face
as if he could already hear
their tires crunching gravel.

Square shouldered, square jawed,
knotty muscles in his arms,
he sat at his desk
all day long, chain smoking
and doodling on a scratch pad
while I did his job and mine,
unloading the trucks that came in
from Alton, Mascoutah and Belleville.

Before he took his afternoon nap,
he warned me to look sharp
and not let Henry catch me dawdling,
but Henry rarely left his air-conditioned office
and when he did, he never made it
anywhere near the loading dock.
"After ten years here," Jerry told me,
"it's my turn to take it easy."

As I hoisted great spools of cloth,
heaved them into the bins,
as sweat ploughed trails
down my face and my eyes stung
with their watery vision,
I wondered what this job
might lead to. On break,

I ate a Nestle's Crunch
and rolled a coke bottle
over my forehead and held it
to my neck before I downed it and threw
it into the alley, where a truck crushed it
beneath its tires, where it became history,
green bits of glass
glinting from the gravel.

MARVIN MILLER GETS HIS SHIRTS

All day he unloads
trucks that back into the dock
from the alley behind Delmar,
then wheels the boxes through the warehouse
and stacks the shelves and tables
with shirts and pants that come
from Taiwan and Singapore, where labor
is "dirt cheap." Mr. Knepf,
a round man with a round
face, who always wears
a blue Ban-lon and dark trousers,
points his finger at the empty
spots and tells him,
"Let's make it snappy."

He sees the customers picking through
the merchandise while Nancy
cranks the cash register
and takes in the bills and makes
change. The light fixtures hum,
the cash register rings
and his dollie clinks and clanks
over the cement floor.
Mr. Knepf is smiling and talking,
making a small fortune
selling brand name
rejects to men who know
a good deal when they see one.

Now the fading light grays
the windows, and as Marvin untangles

the hangers in the clothes cages
and hooks them to the racks,
he watches the men leave
the store with their packages
and cross the street to Fat Hat,
open until 10 p.m..
Mr. Knepf locks the door
and says, "Leave the pants,
but the shirts are all yours."

At the first table he turns over
a blue oxford shirt
with a discoloration barely visible
on the tip of the collar—
two bucks. And under
a pile of messed up shirts,
he finds a Gant
with a slender red thread
in the blue seam of the cuff—
two bucks. And at the next
table back from the window
he picks out an Arrow
with pin stripes and a loose
ivory button—two bucks.
And two bucks more
for the white Hathaway—the prize of the day—
whose mistake even he can't
find, no matter how many
times he turns it over
and holds it up to the light.

WALKING

Less than what we were, we come back
from the quiet of the trees, from dust motes
streaming down through the leaves, from long boulevards
that release their horizon like a blue breath,
back from habits that go on without us,
from signs that wave their dark wands.

The time for us ended long ago
in the gold blaze burning in a puddle,
in the touch of your lips, in the girlish
curve of your body, in the almond-shaped eyes
of the white shepherd shaking itself from sleep
as it rose toward us in the pipe-shop window.
The time for us ended on the path
where the irises dangled their purple tongues
and wasps flew from the tips of cedar bushes,
poking holes in the moist hot air.

Now stoplights blink out their messages.
Raindrops splatter the scaffoldings.
We walk on—green fires flaring at noon.

The Bitterness Of The Prophet

Each night
God sent me visions
that made me shake and twitch
until I burst awake
sweating and feverish
calling out to my mother.

Her presence spread
through my room
like a shadow at dusk.
She warned me
of the cataclysm to come,
then disappeared

without a trace—
not a dent on the couch cushion
or a lipstick smear
on the rim of a glass
or a crumb from the honey cake
she'd been eating.

I feared sleep
and tried to force myself
to stay awake,
sitting upright
and watching tv,
but the second my eyes closed

the apocalypse would begin
and she'd appear in my room
quietly scolding me
for my inability to act.
I told her
it wasn't my fault

if the world fell apart
but she cut me off,
clicking her tongue,
and said she'd never
have given me birth,
never have gone through

what she did for me
if she'd thought
I'd turn out like this,
a man willing
to let the world
go up in smoke

without even lifting
a finger to help.
When I went outside
in the morning,
my neighbors smiled
and waved at me.

They didn't call me names
or throw stones
as she'd predicted.
But wherever I looked
the city became a heap of ruins.
Bodies turned to shapes

imprinted on the walls
or chalked on pavement.
A single crow
flew over the smoke and rubble,
beating back the wind
with its dark wings.

ORPHEUS IN WILLIAMSBURG

If my music would fall
on their ears like rain
drumming the corrugated iron
gates of the chop shop,
if it could be heard
over the boomboxes and the sirens,
over the tattoos roaming
the streets, over the gunshots
and the explosions, over the sobbing,
if it could erase the silhouettes
chalked in yellow
and white on the pavements,
if it could clean
the windows of grief
and raise the gulls
from sleep, mourning
as they circle the tanks,
if it could silence
the crack dealers on the corner
and shut the eyes
of the pit bull chained
to the iron railing under
the blinking neon cross,
then I would play on.
But this is Williamsburg,
not some hell invented
by Greek gods

over 3,000 years ago,
and no one listens
and it doesn't matter
whether I turn toward the
subway or walk on—
nothing can bring her back.

ACHILLES

I smear ashes on my face.
I pour them on my hair
but under your white sheet,
you lie still, your hand
curled on your chest
as though it still clutched a weapon.

When I remember your shining eyes,
like two small birds
perched on a branch,
crunching seeds, I weep.
Even in my armor,
you were not a warrior.

No one approaches my tent
though the gods call me out
to finish what they have started
and your blood, staining rocks
and crushed grass, cries for revenge.

Briseis is the most beautiful
of the all the slave girls,
but I would forsake
her memory—I would
bow down and beg
Agamemnon's forgiveness—
for one more moment with you.

Death claims my heart,
which knows the way
to follow you.
The end of our world
is near, my friend,
even gods turn to dust.

KING DAVID

Five hours a day,
while tending the sheep,
I practiced slinging stones
at a grass spot
marked on the trunk
of a tree. The bark
shattered. The sheep
mulled through the field,
their eyes rimmed red,
like worried patriarchs.
At night in my tent
I didn't dream
of the beautiful women
who would one day
become my lovers.
I didn't dream of
the enormous wealth
I would capture from the Philistines
or the melodies I would pluck
from the strings of my harp
to chase away
the evil spirits
that plagued Saul.
I dreamed of hurling a stone
that would smash
the skull of a warrior
and bring me glory.
When I faced Goliath,
I acted out a scene

I had rehearsed in my mind
a thousand times.
The stone embedded itself
in the giant's forehead
like a final dark thought.
I sliced off his head
with his own sword
and held it up
for God to see.
Only I, David,
greatest king of Israel,
understood his hunger
for human sacrifice, the love
in his murderous heart.

TAKING DOWN THE ANGEL

As he ticked off numbers—
how many sheep
I'd pilfered from Laban
and their rate of reproduction—
he opened and closed
his fists, cracked
his knobby rough-
skinned knuckles.

An angel on the take, I thought,
and he stinks like a goat.
While my white wooly profits
bleated their blessings,
I rose from my perch,
took him down
so hard the breath
went out of him.

He touched the hollow
of my joint and threw
my hip out of whack,
but I put him in
a choke hold he never
escaped from, buried his
crumpled carcass in the hard
white sand.

JOSEPH

In the desert my brothers stripped me
and threw me into a pit. They ripped apart
my coat of many colors
as though destroying the banner
of an enemy nation.

Then they got drunk
laughing as they poured wine
over my head.
My tongue thickened
Speech deserted me.

I felt the desert enter me
through the pupils of my eyes, my mouth,
the pores of my skin.
I grew heavy with sand
and heat.

I thought they might leave me to die
and the hyenas would rip me
apart with their powerful jaws
and the great birds swirling
at the sun would come down

to feed on my intestines
and liver.
When I opened my eyes,
stinging from sweat,
rope bound my wrists.

My feet kept moving.
I heard the asses bray
and the wheels cracking against stone
and the voice of my father
calling from the pit,

Come back, come back.
Ahead lay Egypt
in its blurred dark shine,
salt-hard, bitter, seared
in the fires of my dreaming.

ON THE BANKS OF THE MASCOMA

The water pitched and plunged,
a foamy white swirling to
a froth on the dark rocks
drubbed smooth. You pulled
your hand from mine and went
to sit on a grassy ledge.
Let's not talk, you said
and put your slender fingers to your lips.

I watched a crow burst into flight
and drank bourbon from the bottle
I carried in a paper bag.
The blue of the sky slurred
and a burning gold light
slashed the roiling river.

I wanted to press my ear
to your womb to understand what emptiness
kicked inside you. It was not
for us to hold a child in our arms
or to make the world our little room.

I lay down in the grass for only a moment
but when I woke, shivering, you were gone—
gone from the grass and the purple
wildflowers that dotted the bank,
gone from the slow-moving air,
gone from my hands and arms,
from the touch of my body. From the ledge

I saw the red sign of Kleen Dry Clean
and the cars swerving on 120
toward Longacres and Dulac's Hardware.
I tried to remember all that we had
wanted to become when we imagined a future
as painless as sleep. Over and over
the river splashed against the rocks.
The longer I stared at them,
the smoother they became
and soon even they disappeared.

CONVERSATION
(For Roy Nathanson, Jazz Passengers)

My father sat
in an armchair
day after day
with a striped afghan
over his knees,
unable to remember
his dead wife
or my name
or where he put
his empty wallet
or who phoned him
in 1966
for the biggest
gig of his life.
According to the doc,
he barely lifted
his head anymore,
but when I came in,
the soft dusk
brushed his window
and he pulled out
his clarinet from under
the bed. "How 'bout
a peach?" he asked
and played several
bars of "Embraceable You."
I answered him
with the opening of
"Strange Fruit."
He tapped his foot,

bounced his knee
and lit into
a reedy version
of "In the Mood,"
to which I responded
with a passage from Coltrane's
"My Favorite Things,"
and he countered with "Somebody
to Watch Over Me,"
not even noticing how
the nurse tiptoed
in and gently
closed the door.
"Pop," I said,
"How 'bout that peach,"
and he beamed me a smile.
This is how we talked.

THE FACE

The memory of his father's face
faded a bit more each
day like a blackened patch
of snow receding from a slope.

He was forgetting the smile,
the long furrow of the forehead,
the shade of brown in the iris,
the way sadness or anger composed

his features. He watched the street
pass through its phases of light
and dark and waited for the face
to come back to him

like a full moon
white and heavy in the sky,
but it remained partially in shadow
as if split, two crescent

shaped masses caught
in the instant of their collision.
He picked up the gold cufflinks
his father had given him

and rubbed the raised surfaces
and remembered the strength in his father's
touch, the way he bore down
to open a jar lid

or how he hoisted his heavy grips
from the trunk of the car
and carried them into the house
almost effortlessly.

He remembered the smell of
his father's breath
as he bent down to kiss him
or whisper something,

warm, spicy—
redolent of garlic and scotch.
A rush of hard
consonants burst from his lips.

When the face came clear—
as though the sun had burned through
a thick white ground fog—
his father's voice blended with the sound

of a crow cawing out
from the damp green grass
as it pushed its beak into the earth
and snatched a worm or bread crust.

Then, for a moment, the face
floated in a pool of light
like a paper flower in rain,
and the crow flew off.

JACOB

I survived as the struggle
for power that began
in the womb,
one hand clutching
my brother's heel
to ride into a world
that would destroy everything
we came to love.

I survived as the final blessing
of an old man too blind to see,
who even in death remembered
how his father lifted his blade
to murder him
and the brightness in his eyes
in the heat of noon.

As a birthright
no one is alive to claim,
I survived, as a small bird
beating in the blue air
of a ribbed hollow,
its beak glinting yellow.

I survived as the dank odor of death
rising into the nostrils of the hyena
as it catches its prey by the neck
and rips into the flesh,
and the smell of something bitter
sweeps over the plain.

As the blackness
in the eye of the flame,
as the promise that turned to dust
on the tip of the tongue
and traveled four thousand years
in the wind, I survived,
as the ash drifting over villages
that disappeared long ago.

I survived as the rage
that lived inside you
like breath,
as the unfinished telling
of your bloodiest dreams.

THE SQUATTERS

The iron ball swung
back and forth. The din was so loud
our children held their ears
and trembled as the force of it
vibrated through their bodies.

The building shook
and swayed more violently
with each blow until it buckled
into a mound of bricks.

A light in the distance made
a window on the darkness,
where the dying grail
flickered. While trucks rumbled
over the rubble, a long
tongue deciphered the dust
and debris.

At our feet, a pool grew large
and still, inky with oil.
The statue of our city's protectress
held her eyes shut to the stink.
It was time for us to leave,
time for us to find another
boarded-up building.

A silver trail drilled
through the murderous dusk.
We carried away what we could.

THREE

1965, DUSK
(after Weldon Kees)

I throw a baseball against the stone wall
beneath the window where Kathy Kahn—
22 and not married yet—
fluffs her hair and watches
the road. The scoffed ball
is getting harder to see, but I
snag it and throw again. Across the street

my uncle Eddie Kalachek
walks slowly up and down the block
with his arm around Sylvia Raskas.
They stop and kiss under the sycamores.
As the gnats swirl up from
the green of the lawn, my father
gets out of his silver-gray
Buick Le Sabre and opens
the trunk to carry in his grips.

The air turns a shade darker.
Now I see my father's death
in a car crash on a highway
in Iowa. I see Kathy Kahn
swallow a bottle of sleeping
pills and take her own life.
I see my uncle holding his hands
over his heart as if he could stop it
from failing him, while his young wife
brings him a glass of water.

It is 1965 on this street
where the gnats swirl up
in the blue air, where the sycamores
spread their canopies over the asphalt,
where Kathy Kahn's face
never vanishes from the window
and my uncle and his fiancé hold
each other tenderly, where I run
to hug my father and a smile
spreads over his tired face.

ON THE RIVERFRONT IN ST. LOUIS

At dusk I crouch
on the rocks and stir up
the river with a stick.
A white gravel, the bony

remains of my father,
rises to the surface
and spreads out.
Ash floats toward Granite City.

The clock ticks
over the Eads Bridge.
Trucks rumble
toward Illinois.

The diesel fumes thin.
In the wind
a story is being told,
chimes jangling.

Old clothes wash up.
I taste the dust
and grit that was my father
and spit him back into water.

I smell the scotch
on his breath,
the acetic sweat
that yellowed his shirts,

the Wildroot combed
through his thick curly hair.
He smiles at me—
a briefcase in one hand

and a grip full of sportswear
samples in the other—
and tells me he's going to Chicago,
Minneapolis, then Detroit.

He puts down his samples
for a moment
and we talk about Cardinal baseball,
the bad weather

rolling in from Kansas City,
my mother's health.
"Have you seen my new car?"
he asks. "It's a beaut."

When I turn, I see
a green Buick Riviera
parked on Wharf Street.
"If you travel as much as I do

you need a car
that holds the road."
The shadows deepen
and the car disappears.

My father is gone.
The clouds glow like paper
lamps. The gnats
swirling over the rocks

catch the last red
streaks of sun.
A blue flame
whispers to the river.

LISTENING AT NIGHT

Braced against the brass headrail,
my sister lets her hardback
textbook with its shiny red

spine rest against her chest.
She is learning to study in the dark,
repeating the causes

of the Depression that Mr. Adzick,
her history teacher, outlined
on the blackboard in yellow chalk.

The smell of brisket cooked
in onions lingers in the rooms
of our apartment.

My oldest sister, who has just
pulled both chains of the reading lamp,
bounces the springs of her twin bed

as her body flips over and she pulls
the sheet over her brillo pad
of black hair, pushing into the pillow

spotted with red and yellow flowers.
On the tv in the living room,
the rabbi offers a prayer

to the world before the station goes off
and the high-pitched signal vibrates
through the walls. My father flicks

the channels of the remote, but the static
twitches and jumps. Then the tv
pops off. For a few minutes more

the newspaper cracks and crinkles
until his head droops. Now my sister
fidgets in bed, explaining

Roosevelt's New Deal
under her breath while she waits
for the snoring to begin to snap on

the reading lamp. And in my room
the needle sssts under the turntable arm
as it rides the grooves of the shiny vinyl,

Elvis singing, "You ain't never caught a rabbit
and you ain't no friend of mine . . ."
so softly only I can hear him.

OAK KNOLL

I gave Ronnie Bricker
a dollar to be
my best friend again.

The sun shone
on the plush grass
behind him,

and ducks waddled
out of the pond
shaking drops

from their plump bodies.
We stood outside
Oak Knoll Museum

where replicas of
Tyranosaurus Rex
and Brontosaurus reached up

into the trees
with their mouths open,
their faces hungry.

He held the bill
in the palm of his hand
and stared at it

as if calculating
the number of packs
of baseball cards

or Goldbrick Bars
he could buy with it.
When I saw

his hesitation,
I wanted to sweeten
the deal, to say

"I'll also give you a card
of Stan Musial
and Gene Green," but knew

I couldn't part with them.
"Zeigler's my best friend," he insisted
and gave me back the dollar

and stuffed his hands
in his pockets.
I paid a quarter

to go inside alone,
where I played
TicTacToe

against the computer
for an hour,
but couldn't win,

then rode the bike
that generated electricity
until I finally

pedalled fast enough
to light up
two bulbs.

MR. CLARK'S LAST CLASS

They said he'd crawled out of the trenches
in a hail of enemy fire
to save the lives of two
wounded soldiers, but he looked
effeminate in his pink shirt
and blue blazer, limping from his desk.

As he patrolled the aisle,
I wondered what he thought about
when he stared out the window at the spaces
between the bare sycamores, the snow flurrying
and bursting in mid-air. Did he remember
crawling through the cold mud
to save his friends, the feel
of their wounded flesh against his body?

Did he want to come home
again to the crowds and parades—
ramrod-slim in his uniform—
to dance in the streets as in a newsreel
I had seen? Or did he wish he had never
gone off to the war? He was the only
male teacher
at Glenridge Grade School.

Every hour, he excused himself
to walk down the hall to the fountain.
When the door swung shut
my classmates burst into laughter,
mocking his hawking noises
and mimicking the way he bent over
to deliver his wad of spit
to the shiny white basin.

I sat in the back and watched
the big hand of the clock
tick slowly around the white face
and waited for Mr. Clark
to tell us how he'd become a war hero
or what it means to be brave,
but as the cold winds blew away
the leaves, and snow covered
the tarred blacktop in silence,
he never said a word that seemed to matter.

Soon water dripped
from the drains, the earth thawed,
rivers ran in the streets,
and we went out to play
on the glassy blacktop.
Mr. Clark rose from his desk
and disappeared into the long corridor,
into the crowds of men dancing
in the newsreel, his face shining
as the last glittery shower of confetti
merged with the whiteness of the screen.

MANIFEST DESTINY

Early May, already it is
too warm to wear khakis
and a stiff blue oxford
shirt to school. By 2 p.m.
my shirt gets untucked
and my pants are smudged with crayon,
pencil, eraser shavings.
"Tuck your tails in," Miss Ledbetter
says and turns to the blackboard.
The red bird rustles the cedar branches.
The bluejays take over
the sycamore, gobbling worms.

I lift open my desk
and read the last pages
of my Superboy comic—Clark
is falling in love with
Lana Lang, a red-
haired beauty. I'm falling in
love with Barbie Silverman,
who, the sixth graders say,
has the best legs in the school,
long, slim and smooth
in her blue shorts during
gym class. But she won't
even talk to me.

"Manifest Destiny,"
Miss Ledbetter underlines
the words twice: "The destiny
of Americans to possess
all of America—" like Pressberg
and his friends after school,
taking over the whole playground
for their games, or the crows
usurping the grass, their black
tails wet and shiny,
or my hand moving up and down
Barbie Silverman's bare leg,
which never happens.

FINDING THE ACTION
(For G.C., who died of AIDS)

At Schneithorst's you
tried to pick up
the car hop, a short
blond-haired girl
with buck teeth.
She ignored your comments
and hooked the tray
with our fries and shakes
to the window.
"Look at that—"
You rose up and
pointed at a girl
in a miniskirt
climbing out of the back
seat of a Mustang.
We could see the red
polka dots
on her panties
and the backs of her
long golden legs.
I put my hand
on your shoulder
and pulled you back.
"I want to get
laid real bad,"
you said.

Winding through
the narrow lanes
and curvy roads

past long rows
of neatly trimmed
hedges, stone
statues, timed
sprinklers flinging
hard drops
of water toward
the sloping edges
of lawn, we drove
to the Holmes' house,
but Nan's windows
were dark. "No action
here," I said.

At the Jewel Box
in Forest Park
we sat in the car
with the doors open
and finished the last
of a bottle of Sloe Gin,
stolen from your
father's liquor cabinet.
"Have you ever had
a really good
blow job?"
I was almost afraid
to look at you, afraid
to stare into the shining

wedge of your face.
"I can give you
a blow job," you said,
"that will send you through
the roof of the car."
How could I have prevented you
from saying what you felt
or stopped us from
growing apart?

I thought of the exotic
flowers behind the glass
walls, releasing
their perfume to the dark,
how the fragrant scents
grow so potent
they make a new
kind of air,
thick with sweetness,
how jewels form
on the palms of the fibrous
green leaves
that sparkle
only a moment
before they burst.

Under the thick canopy
of the sycamores, their

trunks lit
by a milky flame,
I looked at your stained
lips, your palms
opening and closing.
Then I shoved the clutch
into gear and patched out
on the tarry road
and sticking my head out
the window, laughed
into the warm buggy
wind rushing into
my eyes and mouth.

WORKING THE LOADING DOCK AT FAMOUS-BARR

Before 9 a.m.
I heard the hum of horseflies
and the first trucks pounding
the entrance ramp to the delivery
dock at Famous-Barr.
My t-shirt damp, clinging
to my belly and back, I carried
milk crates to The Lamplight Room
and pushed tall silver carts—
shelved with trays of sugar
cookies in the shape of hearts,
brownies dotted with nuts, and hard
rolls—to the bakery.

In the bins Cordell
and Joe, lifers on the job,
rolled a joint as thick
as Cordell's thumb and lit up
while I ripped open boxes and grabbed
handfuls of M&Ms and sunflower seeds
leaving a trail of shells
wherever I went.
The smell of marijuana
lingered on the loading dock,
mixing with the dust from the alley
and the smell of hot asphalt.

"Take it slow," Cordell said
and put his warm heavy hand
on my shoulder and opened his mouth
into a smile that showed his chipped
front teeth and large eyeteeth.
When the afternoon trucks delivered
their cargoes of tvs, stereos,
fans, air-conditioners and housewares,
I unloaded them alone. The smoke
grew thick over the empty
loading dock, and high above me
horseflies spun their heavy
orbits in the dark of the rafters.

BOWLING INSTRUCTION

"Aim at the second
arrow," Ken said
and approached the alley
with long graceful steps.

I hoped his ball
would, for once, careen
into the gutter, but he swung
his right arm back

until it reached the peak
of a perfect arc
and whipped forward
as though sprung from a catch,

just before the release
flicking his wrist.
The ball cracked
against the floor, hooked

into the pocket,
hitting just above
the lead pin,
and sent all 10 pins

crashing into the catcher.
A warm red flush
spread over his face,
and I wanted to match

his sense of self satisfaction,
to show him I could
do it too.
"You're up," he said.

I held my hands together
and blew into them
like someone trying
to spark a flame in a grill,

and remembered
what he taught me,
the crouch, the stance,
the release—a deft

stroke in the air.
When I uncoiled my arm
the ball didn't hook
enough, broke

the pocket too high,
and down the long alley
three pins stood—
a wide split.

"It's all technique,"
he bobbed his head
and smiled while the cage
of the pin setter lifted

and the spotted blue
ball rose
through the return hole
into my outstretched hand.

POEM FOR LARRY LEVIS

You turned your cigarette upside down
and breathed on its glowing tip
and watched it burn.
Then you walked to the window and stared out
without speaking. I had never seen a teacher
turn his back on a class
for such a long time.

Did you see the gray smoke
curling over the low flat
buildings, the bodies sprawled
on the green, the black stripe
of asphalt that crosses a continent?

Did you remember the grapes
thickening on vines, how you reached out
with your curved knife and cut
the stems and dropped the tight
bunches into the metal pail,
how you bit slowly into the hard skins
to hold the sweet juice on your tongue
until you could no longer taste it?

Did you hear the migrant workers humming
in the vineyards of Malaga or the sounds
of our unformed poems floating down
over the pavement like white feathers?

When you came back to us, the sun
fell on the right side of your face
and your green eyes flared
beneath heavy brows
and you read each of our poems
with such intensity
that all of us believed our words
had been struck by some blazing light.
I couldn't imagine where your power
came from, for when you sat back down
you seemed so world weary
slouched in your chair, your eyes
were barely able to look at us.

Then you lit another cigarette,
puckered your lips and blew
smoke rings out over the class
and watched them curl and stretch
and break open and when you spoke
the glowing tip of your cigarette
burned your words into the air
and you rose once more to show us
where poetry might live,
threaded through our dreams and flowing
from the heart, quietly ticking
its own lovely, mortal rhythm.

BURP WATER

A sour look on his face,
his trousers loosened, my father
takes a bill out of his pockets
and hands it to me. "Make yourself

useful, Junior. You just got
time to make it to the store."
I run out of the apartment and take
the steps in a single leap.

I run through a cloud of gnats
humming over the pavement, through
the cedar hedges—green
needles embed themselves in my arms—

through the spray of the sprinkler, drops
streaking my glasses so everything
looks watery, past the streetlamps just
blinking on, past the baggers collecting

grocery carts and pushing them up
the freshly tarred blacktop,
painted with yellow lines,
into a blast of cold air

as the automatic door swings open.
The counter, where some days I swivel
the stools and sip cherry cokes
or dip a shiny spoon into a seventeen cent

hot fudge sundae, is closed.
Cashiers thumb
the bills in the black trays
of their cash registers as they add up

the money and stuff it in pouches.
"Burp Water," I say
and a plump lady in a blue
Bettendorf's outfit laughs

and repeats the words, "Burp
Water," as if they might work some
magic and reaches up high
to get a fat bottle of D.C. Club Soda.

At home I give my father
the change, which he drops
in his deep, loose pockets.
He screws off the bottle cap

and watches the Club Soda
fizz, before taking a big
swig—the sourness already
disappearing from his fleshy face.

"Burp water," I say
and he lets out a belch that shakes the
chandelier over the dinner table.
He is young and handsome again,

ready to take on the world
with his wide fleshy smile,
a few good wisecracks,
and a helluva sales pitch.

Upstairs, Mrs. Handshear stops
running the vacuum cleaner
over her wood floors and sings
Madame Butterfly in falsetto.

Strings of shells, picked from
the sands of Miami Beach, clink
against each other in the doorway
of Mr. Lamar's apartment

and rip from their nails. My father
tells me how much he will make
on his next sales trip,
how he will buy a navy blue Buick

Riviera with all the gadgets.
"Burp water," I say—
fizzing bubbles pop and burst.
A newspaper over his face, he falls into

a loud slumber on the couch,
dreaming of hidden headlights
and automatic door locks,
while my mother looks in the mirror,

rubs white cream
into the faint lines on her forehead,
and my sister touches her delicate
straight nose as she waits by

the black telephone on her nightstand—
which only she can use—
hoping a boy will call for a date.
"Burp water—" I play

poker against myself
on the living room floor
and turn over the winning hand,
kings over threes, a full house.

I TALK TO MY FATHER TEN YEARS AFTER HIS DEATH

Dad, I never liked Branding Iron.
and Mrs. Hullings Cafeteria
might have been good at one time
but after she sold the place

it went downhill fast. And the Sunday brunch
at the Cheshire Inn, with a choice
of 32 different dishes, isn't
what it used to be either.

Ruggeri's closed down
about ten years ago, and your favorite waiter,
Charlie, who made sure your prime rib
was cooked rare and served

with a baked potato and no other
vegetables on the plate, retired,
but still does the charity raffle.
Thank God mother no longer feels

obligated to donate.
And Earl White sank down in the office
of his service station
like a deflated innertube

and never rose up again
to ring up a total on the cash register.
Steve at the Chase Park Plaza—
who cut your hair so poorly

your head looked like a lopsided egg—
went out of business a while back.
I think you were the last of his regulars.
Sometime after the accident

Mother had a big apartment sale
at Oxford Hills and sold off
your golf clubs, electric razors,
green canvas grips,

the color tv
and a dozen ballpoint pens,
then she moved into a
security building near Culpeppers,

a small apartment
with a screened-in porch
and a nice view out the back
of a fountain with colored lights.

I don't know what to tell you about myself
except I didn't turn out like
Bobby Caprini Jr. and I'm not
so good at making a buck.

IN THE KINGDOM OF MY PALM

From far away
my mother calls out to me,
a thread of voice
that floats through air,

words breathed
into the darkness.
Near death
she sits in a room

with all her things
and calls out to me
with her hands curled
like irises,

with the pain spreading
along the ridges of her shoulders,
with the soft touch
of her tongue on her lips.

She wants me
to come back to her
before she closes her eyes,
before she lies down

and gives up her body
to dust and ash.
She calls out to me
from the blue blush of light,

from the swirl of molecules
colliding in the kingdom
of my palm, from the roads
that rip through me.

I am the son
who kicked his feet
and splashed in the dark waters
of her womb, and made her cry.

I am the son she set into motion
like a small planet orbiting around her,
the son she taught
to lift a spoon and eat.

Now a wind enters her room.
The metal chimes jangle.
The gold swans
reach toward the flames.

I sit with her one last time,
close her eyes
with my fingertips,
and call her "mother."

VIGIL

When you tremble in sleep
and cry out and rise
from your pillow
as though trying to escape
something horrible
I slip my arms
around you and hold you
until I can gently
lay you back down.

For a moment your eyes
struggle to stay
open—the blue
irises flecked
with white—then they relent
and the lids close over them.

The tv plays
without sound. Tanks
roll through a decimated city.
The countryside goes up
in a blaze.

The faces of those who have
lost limbs
or been badly burned
stare straight up
at sky or ceiling.
Who can survive such pain?

It will not be long
until the shade turns
a light blue
and the first birds
whisper their songs.

You must go deeper
into sleep to bury your fear
for soon we must rise like breath
into the bright brutal world
that never meant to do us
any good.

RECITAL

The tv's on the blink again.
My father hits it with the palm
of his hand and jiggles
the bent hanger that serves
as an aerial, but the images
won't come clear. Finally he
utters his surrender, "phooey,"
and turns the volume knob
to zero and sits down with a disgusted
look on his face. Another
year of declining sales
and now this . . .

Small and dark, my sister
walks out of the wings with her sheet music
and takes her place at the piano bench.
After several years of lessons
she plays only one piece, "Malaguena,"
a choppy off-key interpretation
that rivals in quality her vocal
rendition of "Getting to Know You."

With her legs crossed my mother
sits on the edge of the couch,
attentive, as though at a real concert—
she does not hold her chest
or slump down in pain—while I lie
on the floor staring at the screen
hoping that the picture will unfuzz
or that the phone will ring. My sister's

100

hands lift over the keyboard,
her face caught in the grip
of concentration. She is young and pretty
with firm pointy breasts
that press against her knit shirt.
Cancer is just a word she has
looked up in the dictionary or heard about
in school. The veins fan out
on the backs of her hands as they come
down hard and quick on the keys.

The sound of "Malagueña" fills the room
and I hold their faces in my memory
a moment longer. The tv's on the blink.
My sister leans into the piano.
My mother smiles. My father
dozes off on a long, hot night.